This is one of a series of books on modern art created to help very young people learn the basic vocabulary used by artists, a sort of ABC of art. Parents and teachers play a key role in this learning process, encouraging careful, thoughtful looking. This book isolates shapes to show how they are used by artists and how they contribute to meaning in art. By looking at shapes and discussing what ideas and feelings they suggest, adults encourage children to develop creative thinking skills. At the back of this book, there is more information about the pictures included to help in this engaging process.

Enjoy looking together!

# Shapes

**Philip Yenawine**

**The Museum of Modern Art, New York**
**Delacorte Press**

Acknowledgements
This book was made possible by the generosity of The Eugene and
Estelle Ferkauf Foundation; John and Margot Ernst; David Rockefeller,
Jr.; John and Jodie Eastman; Joan Ganz Cooney; and The Astrid Johansen
Memorial Gift Fund. Of equal importance where the talents of Takaaki
Matsumoto, Michael McGinn, Mikio Sakai, David Gale, Harriet Bee,
Richard Tooke, Mikki Carpenter, Nancy Miller, Alexander Gray, Carlos
Silveira, and particularly Catherine Grimshaw. I am extremely grateful to
all of them.

Library of Congress Cataloging in Publication Data

Yenawine, Philip.
Shapes/by Philip Yenawine.
        p.        cm.
Summary: Isolates the artistic element of shape, discusses what
visual ideas and effects can be conveyed by different shapes, and exam-
ines how they contribute to a work of art through various examples from
The Museum of Modern Art in New York.
ISBN 0-385-30255-X (trade ed.). –ISBN 0-385-30315-7 (lib. ed.)
1. Form perception–Juvenile literature.   [1. Form perception.
2. Shape. 3. Art appreciation.]   I. Title.
N7430.5. Y46 1991
701'.1–dc20   90-38985   CIP   AC

ISBN 0-87070-177-0 (MoMA)


The Museum of Modern Art
11 West 53 Street
New York, NY 10019

Delacorte Press
Bantam Doubleday Dell Publishing Group, Inc.
666 Fifth Avenue
New York, New York 10103

Printed in Italy

# Some pictures are made only of shapes.

Georges-Pierre Seurat, *At the "Concert Européen"*

1

Some artists paint shapes of things they see. Name the things you see here. How many groups of three can you find? Can you find any hidden shapes?

Paul Gauguin, *Still Life with Three Puppies*

# The shapes can be very simple.

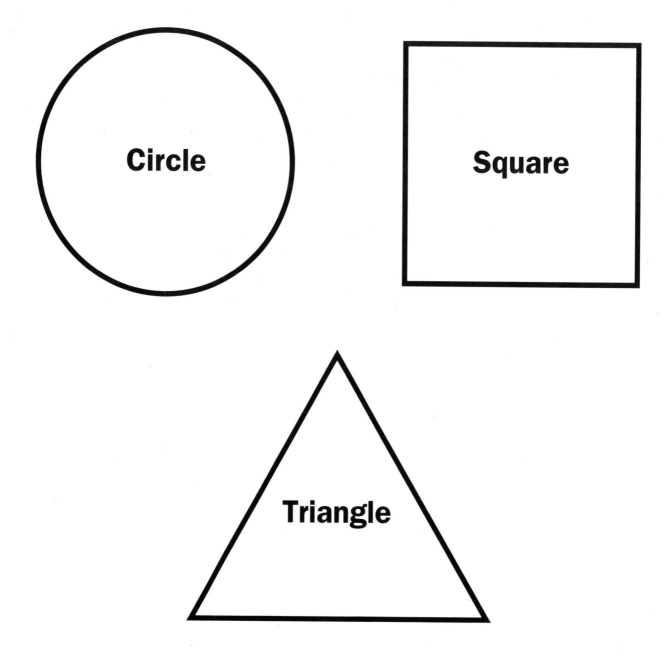

Circle

Square

Triangle

# The fun then is deciding where to put them.

Kasimir Malevich, *Suprematist Element: Circle;* Kasimir Malevich, *Suprematist Elements: Squares*

# Sometimes the shapes are exact.

Piet Mondrian, *Composition*

# Sometimes they aren't.

Jean (Hans) Arp, *Arrangement According to the Laws of Chance (Collage with Squares)*

# This is a picture made of many tiny squares. What other shapes can you find?

Paul Klee, *Castle Garden*

# Sometimes the shapes don't look like anything special, so you can imagine whatever you want. What can you imagine about these?

David Smith, *Untitled (Tanktotems)*

**With a few lines an artist**

**turns a circle into a ball.**

**Or into a cylinder shaped like a cup.**

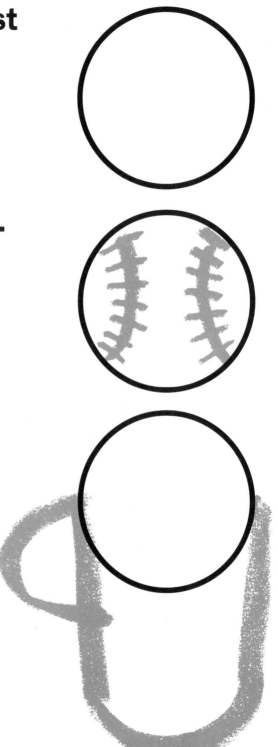

# Here's a picture using balls and cylinders. Can you find them?

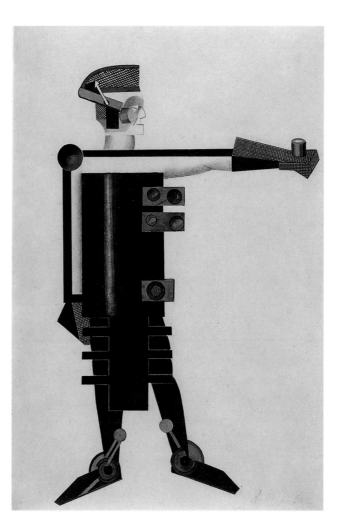

Aleksandra Exter, Costume design for *The Guardian of Energy*

# Artists also turn squares into boxes or buildings.

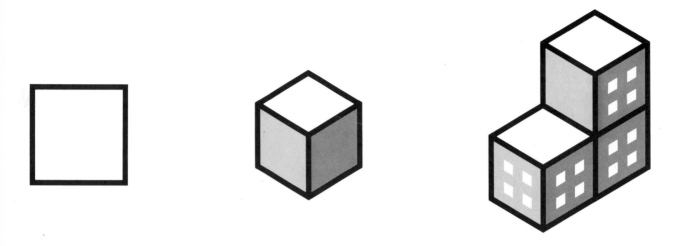

# And a triangle into a pyramid or a roof.

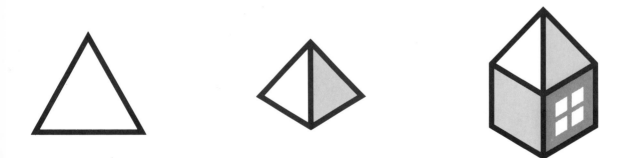

# Can you find buildings? And roofs?

Pablo Picasso, Study for *The Mill at Horta*

**Using shadows and shading, artists turn shapes into forms.**

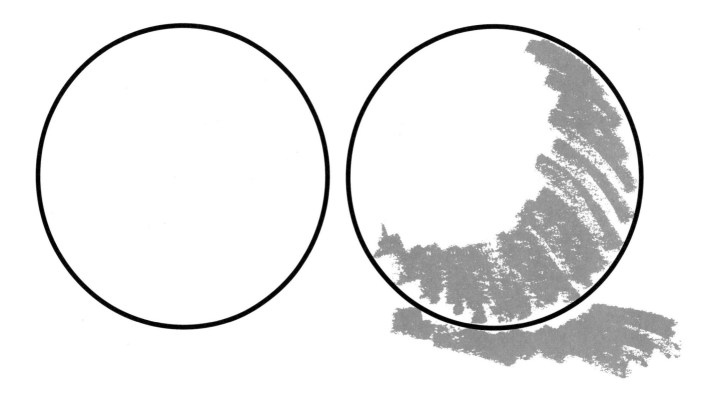

# See how the artist used shadows and shading to make the feet in these drawings seem real?

Salvador Dali, Detail from *Studies of a Nude*

**These three lines can help us imagine the shape of a whole room.**

**This man seems to be standing in a room with a window. Behind his arm there is a table with a pitcher.**

George Grosz, *The Engineer Heartfield*

**Can you find a bowl in this picture? A table?
Can you name the fruit you see?
Can you find light areas and dark shadows?**

Paul Cézanne, *Still Life with Apples*

# Can you also find circles, squares, triangles, and a cylinder?

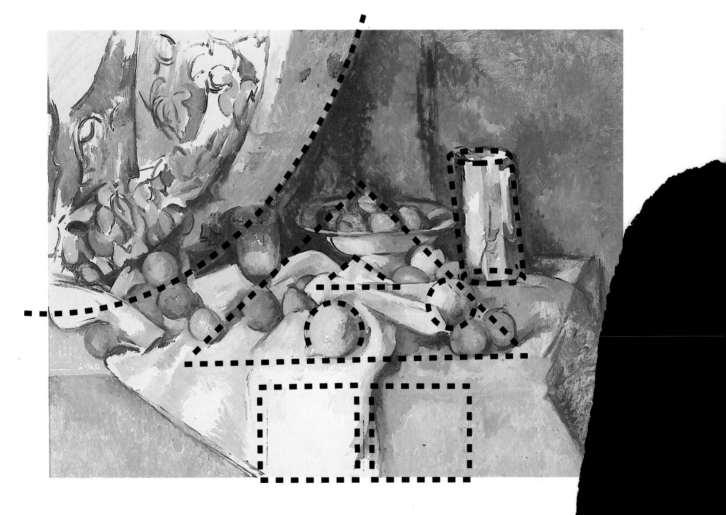

You can spend a long time finding shapes in this picture:

triangles and circles,

the shapes of masks and mustaches,

a guitar and funny little hands,

d many more.

you find a dog?

t forget his tail and his furry body.

Pablo Picasso, *Three Musicians*

Maybe you would like to make some
drawings of your own using shapes.
Big and little ones. Neat and messy ones.
Shapes of things you can see.
Imaginary shapes. Shapes with shadows.

The art in this book can be found at The Museum of Modern Art in New York City. Other museums and galleries have many interesting pictures too, and it is good to make a habit of visiting them, looking for shapes. You can also look in magazines, books, buildings, parks, and gardens.

Page 1

Georges-Pierre Seurat
*At the "Concert Européen,"* 1887–88
Conte crayon, chalk, and gouache on paper
12 1/4 x 9 3/8" (31.1 x 23.9 cm)
Lillie P. Bliss Collection

Seurat depicted forms without using outlines, emphasizing that the lines upon which most artistic creation depends do not exist in nature.

Page 3

Paul Gauguin
*Still Life with Three Puppies*, 1888
Oil on wood
36 1/8 x 24 5/8" (91.8 x 62.6 cm)
Mrs. Simon Guggenheim Fund

Gauguin's works often intrigue us because they are not only visually appealing but also a little mysterious. For example, the viewpoint is strange here and the combination of objects is illogical.

age 5

Kasimir Malevich
*Suprematist Element: Circle,* 1915
Pencil on paper
18 1/2 x 14 3/8" (47 x 36.5 cm)

Malevich felt that social ideals could be expressed in art. For example, simple geometric forms arranged in various ways could suggest differing relationships between individual units and the whole.

Page 5

Kasimir Malevich
*Suprematist Elements: Squares,* 1915
Pencil on paper
19 3/4 x 14 1/4" (50.2 x 35.8 cm)

Page 6

Piet Mondrian
*Composition*, 1933
Oil on canvas
16 1/4 x 13 1/8" (41.2 x 33.3 cm)
The Sidney and Harriet Janis Collection

To Mondrian, arranging and rearranging very simple elements— black lines and rectangles of white, red, blue, or yellow—was a way of creating pictures that achieved ideal harmonies.

Page 7

Jean (Hans) Arp
*Arrangement According to the Laws of Chance (Collage with Squares),* 1916–17
Torn and pasted papers on paper
19 1/8 x 13 5/8" (48.6 x 34.6 cm)
Purchase

Arp dropped torn paper squares, observed the pattern in which they fell, and then reproduced that pattern in his picture. He hoped to remove conscious decision-making, and thus find some natural truth.

**Page 8**

Paul Klee
*Castle Garden,* 1931
Oil on canvas
26 1/2 x 21 5/8" (67.2 x 54.9 cm)
Sidney and Harriet Janis Collection
Fund

Klee borrowed the form of mosaics
to construct this image, something a
child might emulate on graph paper.

**Page 9**

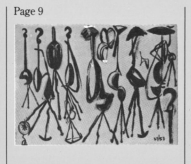

David Smith
*Untitled (Tanktotems),* 1953
Brush and ink, and gouache on
paper
29 3/4 x 42 3/8" (75.6 x 107.5 cm)
Gift of Alexis Gregory

Smith is best known for his abstract
sculptural forms, many of which
seem to refer to nature, as these
figures do.

**Page 11**

Aleksandra Exter
Costume.design for *The Guardian of
Energy,* 1924
Pen and ink, gouache, and pencil on
paper
21 1/4 x 14 1/4"(51.1 x 36 cm)
The J. M. Kaplan Fund, Inc.

Exter created industrial-looking
armor to symbolize, through the
authority of knights, the power
of today's energy sources.

**Page 13**

Pablo Picasso
Study for *The Mill at Horta,* 1909
Watercolor on paper
9 3/4 x 15" (24.8 x 38.2 cm)
The Joan and Lester Avnet
Collection

One aspect of Picasso's Cubism is
to simplify shapes found in nature,
reducing them to geometric forms.

**Page 15**

Salvador Dali
*Studies of a Nude,* 1935
Pencil on paper
6 7/8 x 5 1/2" (17.5 x 14 cm)
The James Thrall Soby Bequest

To Dali, probing mysteries beyond
the obvious involved learning to
create extremely believable illusions
of reality.

**Page 17**

George Grosz
*The Engineer Heartfield,* 1920
Watercolor, pasted postcard, and
halftone on paper
16 1/2 x 12" (41.9 x 30.5 cm)
Gift of A. Conger Goodyear

The cell-like space of this room
serves to intensify the fierce
determination of the man's face
and pose.

**Page 18**

Paul Cézanne
*Still Life with Apples,* 1895–98
Oil on canvas
27 x 36 1/2" (68.6 x 92.7 cm)
Lillie P. Bliss Collection

Cézanne saw painting not as
depicting nature but as a set
of visual problems, important in
themselves–emphasizing the
canvas's flatness to set up spatial
ambiguities, for example.

**Page 21**

Pablo Picasso
*Three Musicians,* 1921
Oil on canvas
6' 7" x 7' 3 3/4"(200.7 x 222.9 cm)
Mrs. Simon Guggenheim Fund

Other aspects of Cubism include
flattening of space and forms,
in general, and employing a narrow
range of colors.